JEWELRY FOR ALL SEASONS

JEWELRY FOR

24 bead and wire designs to make, inspired by nature

ALL SEASONS

Linzi Alford

First published 2014 by
Guild of Master Craftsman
Publications Ltd
Castle Place
166 High Street
Lewes
East Sussex BN7 1XU

Text and illustrations
© Linzi Alford, 2014
Copyright in the Work
© GMC Publications Ltd, 2014

ISBN 978 1 86108 956 4

A catalog record for this book is
available from the British Library.

Set in DIN and Arrus
Color origination by GMC
Reprographics
Printed and bound in China

Publisher: Jonathan Bailey
Production Manager: Jim Bulley
Managing Editor: Gerrie Purcell
Senior Project Editor: Sara Harper
Editor: Nicola Hodgson
Managing Art Editor: Gilda Pacitti
Photographers: Linzi Alford and
Rebecca Mothersole
Designer: Ali Walper

CONTENTS

Introduction   6

Equipment and techniques

Tools   10

Materials   14

Practical information

Inspiration and planning   22

Wrapped loops and
     connectors   24

Hook and eye clasps   26

Crimps   28

Shrink plastic   30

Molds and casts   32

Resin   36

Dye oxide paints   38

The Projects

SPRING

Spring inspirations   40

Daffodil necklace   44

Pink blossom bracelet   48

Magnolia necklace   52

Bleeding heart bracelet   56

Bluebell bracelet   60

Forget-me-not necklace   64

SUMMER

Summer inspirations   70

Bee and aquilegia necklace   74

Buttercups and daisies
     bracelet   78

Dragonfly woods necklace   82

Storm clouds necklace   88

Rose cameo choker   94

Butterflies and thistles
     tiara   100

FALL

Fall inspirations   104

Sunset bracelet   108

Dandelion wishes pendant   112

Frozen rose bracelet   116

Fruits and berries lariat   120

Fall leaves bracelet   124

Oak leaf and acorns
     necklace   130

WINTER

Winter inspirations   136

Snowy holly bag charm   140

Frozen berries necklace   144

Hoar frost necklace   148

Spiderweb necklace   154

Forsythia brooch   158

Snowdrop earrings   162

Suppliers 166 • Acknowledgments 166 • Index 167

INTRODUCTION

THE IDEA FOR WRITING this book came to me after several years of taking photographs cataloguing the changing seasons, capturing the flowers and scenery around me. I am lucky enough to live in England's Lake District, where there is no shortage of natural beauty for inspiration. I wanted to mark the progress of the seasons by designing a range of jewelry that reflected the natural world throughout the year, complete with the photographs

that influenced them. To me, jewelry-making is an obsession rather than just a hobby, and I never tire of dreaming up new designs. Translating those ideas into something stylish and wearable, from the concept through to the actual construction, and having the satisfaction of seeing an imagined piece made into an item to be worn or given as a gift is very gratifying.

In this comprehensive step-by-step guide, you will learn how to master the techniques that will enable you to produce unique and fabulous pieces of jewelry as beautiful and as exuberant as the natural world

that inspired them. Most projects are easy enough for a beginner to tackle, but hopefully will also spark the imagination of the more experienced maker.

Materials are listed for each project, but feel free to adapt any design and substitute your favorite beads, or try changing a project's color scheme for a totally fresh look. If you are a complete beginner then persevere—practice really does make perfect, and from those first tentative, wobbly loops will come beautifully neat wire wraps, together with a real sense of achievement.

If I had to choose just one favorite photo, it would be *"Bee and Aquilegia"* on page 74. There is just something about the lighting that personifies summer to me. I hope that you will be inspired by your own favorite photograph, and that you enjoy reading this book and making the projects as much as I have enjoyed writing it.

Linzi

EQUIPMENT AND TECHNIQUES

In this section you will find the basic techniques needed for creating unique pieces of jewelry. For professional results, always practice the techniques thoroughly, and familiarize yourself with any tools or supplies you've not used before.

TOOLS

You will not need many jewelry-making tools to get going; you can start with a basic cheap set and add to it and upgrade as you go. The core tools that I use in almost every project are chain-nose pliers, flat-nose pliers, round-nose pliers, bent-nose pliers, and wire cutters. These are always on my workbench and are my can't-manage-without basics. Here we also look at other, more specialist, tools that are used for the projects in this book.

1 Chain-nose pliers

These have pointed ends to the jaws and are very versatile.

2 Flat-nose pliers

These are similar to chain-nose pliers, but have wider and flatter jaws.

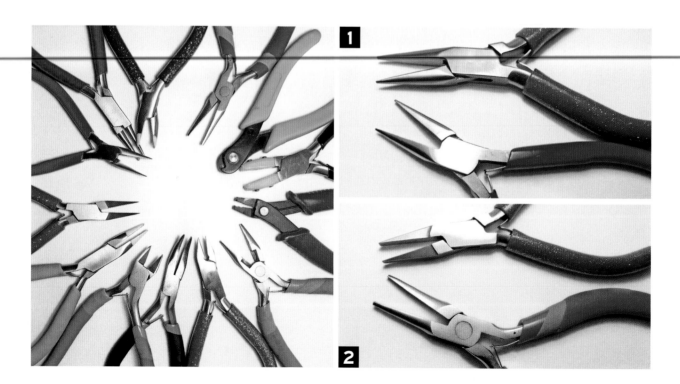

3 Round-nose pliers

These have graduated round-shaped jaws and are used for forming loops and rings. Draw a line on the jaw with permanent marker if you want to make a number of loops exactly the same size.

4 Bent-nose pliers

These are useful for the wrapping part of wrapped loops (see page 24), and for working in small spaces where longer jaws can't reach.

5 Wire cutters

Used to cut wire, the pointed jaws on this tool ensure that wire is closely snipped.

6 Memory wire cutters

These cutters should be used only to cut memory wire, as this tough wire will mar the jaws of ordinary cutters.

7 Nylon jaw pliers

The smooth, soft, nylon pads of these pliers are useful for straightening wire lengths by pulling them through the jaws, and for less detailed work where you don't want to mark metal. Usually the pads can be replaced once worn down.

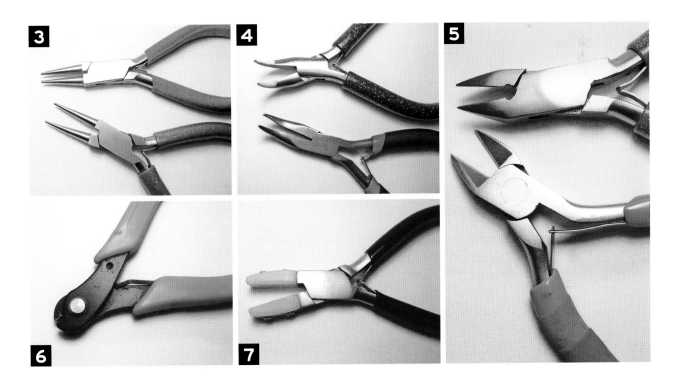

8 Crimp pliers

These pliers have two sections: one to flatten crimps and the other to fold and shape them.

You may notice that some of my pliers have a rubber coating on the jaws; this is to prevent them from scratching coated colored wires. They can be peeled off and replaced as needed.

9 Hole punches

Another useful tool is a hole punch—both the screw type for thicker-gauged metals, and the pliers type for thinner gauges.

10 Chain Sta grips or third hand clip stand

These tools are used for holding work still and for providing an extra pair of hands. They are especially good for projects when you are attaching a lot of charms or dangles to chain or bracelet blanks.

11 Heat gun

Emitting much gentler heat than a blowtorch, this type of crafting heat gun can be used for embossing and heating metals. Be warned that it will get hot enough to heat patina metal and will melt, distort, or burn small items, so take the appropriate protective measures for surfaces when using this tool.

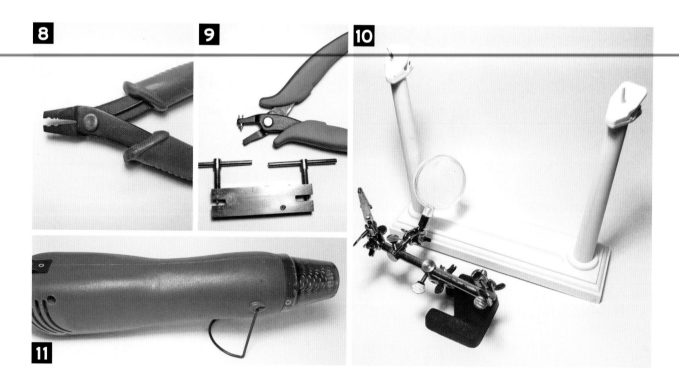

8

9

10

11

12 Soldering block

This is a heatproof block used for protecting surfaces when using a heat gun or blowtorch. Made from a lightweight non-asbestos material, it will retain heat for some time afterward.

13 Heatproof cloth

A heatproof cloth or mat, made from glass fiber, should be used when soldering or using a heat gun. I like to use this under a soldering block for extra protection of the table. The fabric can be spiky to touch due to the glass fibers.

14 Tweezers

Bent- and straight-nose reverse-action soldering tweezers are used to move and hold small pieces while heating metal. The jaws work in reverse so they open when squeezed; this means you can use them to hold work without having to hold the tweezers closed. They have insulated handles to protect your fingers from heat.

Brass tweezers are non-magnetic and, when used during soldering, do not react to acid.

MATERIALS

You don't need a vast stash of supplies to get started in jewelry-making. However, if you are anything like me, an inner magpie takes over and there is never such a thing as enough. Nevertheless, you can start creating with just a few basics and essentials. Here is a short rundown of the different materials you might use; I could fill an entire book describing every variation. Browse in your favorite bead store or search online to see the true extent of the treasures available and the "things you won't know you need until you see them."

Findings

Findings are the "nuts and bolts" of jewelry-making. They are often not the shiniest or prettiest items, but are very important.

1 HEADPINS

These are usually between 1³⁄₁₆ and 2in (30–50mm) long. They can have pin-type ends, balls, or eyepins with a loop. These heads function as a stopper for beads; the other end is usually turned into a loop for attaching to your project. They are available in different gauges; for example, a pearl would need a thin-gauge headpin.

2 JUMPRINGS

Available in a variety of sizes and colors, these have many purposes, such as attaching charms to chain. Always open a jumpring using two pairs of pliers: twist the two sides away sideways, one toward you and one away, rather than pulling them apart outward, as this makes them difficult to close and distorts the round shape. Chain links also make great jumprings.

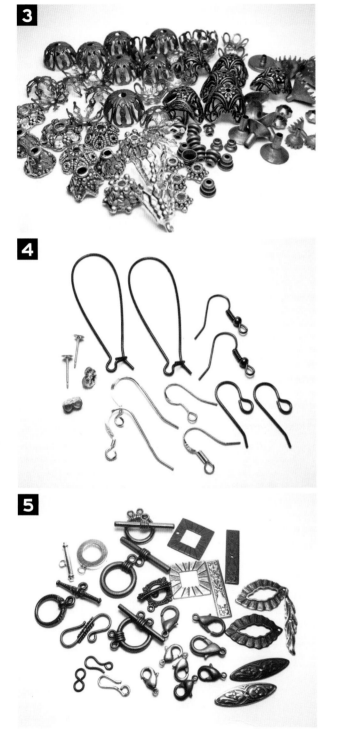

3 BEAD CAPS

Used to enclose beads, bead caps come in many different sizes and styles, from very large and ornate to tiny and plain. I used some fancy Art Nouveau-style bird and beehive bead caps to enhance the Dragonfly woods necklace, for example (see pages 82–87).

4 EARRING FINDINGS

Although it is easy to make your own ear wires, earring findings are widely available and inexpensive to buy.

5 CLASPS AND CONNECTORS

A feature clasp makes all the difference to a project, but the humble lobster or parrot clasp are also very useful and secure. Toggle and loop clasps are easy to fasten, but are not adjustable.

Connectors are usually made of metal, although sometimes come in polymer clay or other materials. They have a hole on each end to which jumprings and other components can be attached. They come in different styles; for example, I used "dog bone" connectors in the Frozen berries necklace (see pages 144–147).

Measurements: While the conversions from metric to imperial are as accurate as possible, it is always best to stick to one system or the other throughout a project.

Chains, wire, and other materials for stringing

You can use many different materials as the basis for your wire and bead jewelry, from conventional ones such as chain, wire, and ribbon, to more unusual choices such as hemp, rubber, or suede.

1 CHAIN

Rolo, scroll, flat, book, ladder, flat and double-link, curb and peanut are just some of the many different types of chain. Different sizes of chain are available, from large-linked and oversize to tiny and delicate, and they come in all metals and plated finishes.

2 WIRE

Wire is available in a vast array of colors, thicknesses (called "gauges"), shapes (round, square, and half-round), and metals. Most of the colored wires are coated copper; care needs to be taken not to damage the coating while working with it.

Silver- and gold-plated wire is inexpensive and is widely available, although the plating will eventually wear off to reveal the pink copper beneath.

Solid metal wire in copper, brass, or sterling silver is more costly—practice a project first using cheaper wire before using sterling silver. Aluminum wire is cheap and lightweight.

Memory wire is supplied in coils. It is very hard and springy, and holds its shape; because memory wire is made with hardened steel it requires special cutters (see page 11).

3 STRINGING AND KNOTTING MATERIALS

Beading wire is a multi-strand stainless-steel wire that has a nylon coating. It is available in different strand thicknesses; 7-strand is the thinnest but weakest and 21-strand is thicker, stronger, and more flexible. The strand thickness needed will depend on the size and weight of beads being strung. Designs made using beading wire are usually finished off with crimps (see pages 28–29).

Monofilament, also known as invisible thread, is thin nylon beading thread. It is similar to fishing line.

Beading needles have a large eye that is collapsible to enable it to pass through bead holes. These needles are often long, very thin, and constructed of very fine twisted wire.

4 RIBBON

You can use every type of width and color of ribbon in your projects. I am a big fan of sari ribbon, made from offcuts from sari silk factories, with its unstructured, frayed edges. Dyed silk ribbon, multicolored gypsy ribbon, satin, and organza ribbon are also great for adding an extra dimension to your designs.

Adhesives and sealants

There are many types of glue that can be used in jewelry-making. Here is a quick rundown of the most suitable types that I have used in the projects in this book.

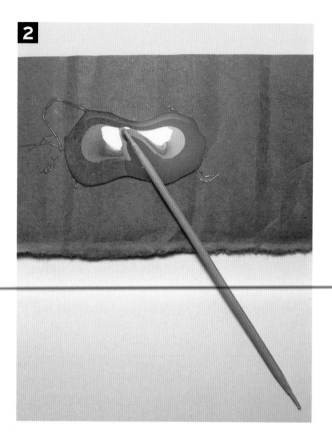

1 SUPER GLUE OR CYANOACRYLATE

This is a fast-acting glue; it sticks everything, including your fingers! It is useful for preventing knots from coming undone or fastening a bead into place, but it can leave a mark on metal that takes the shine away. The glue join can be brittle so it is not suitable for gluing components together.

2 TWO-PART EPOXY GLUE

This is the type that comes in two tubes (one of hardener and one of resin) that you need to mix together in equal quantities. I mix this on a piece of scrap card using a cocktail stick. Leave the stick in the leftover mixed glue on the card; if it sets hard you know the join will be secure.

Some types set in as little as five minutes. If mixed in the correct proportions, this glue gives a very solid join and works on metal and glass. It smells strong so you will need good ventilation.

Always sand items slightly with fine sandpaper before joining to provide a roughened area to give the glue something to grip to. Also make sure that items are free from grease or oil. Some types of glue can affect the foil backs on stones and even melt acrylic beads, so research your material and chosen glue first to avoid disasters.

I would be remiss if I did not remind you to wear gloves and safety glasses when using materials that can splash, get hot, or when you are mixing resin or resin clay. Always work in a well-ventilated room when using glue, heat, or resin.

3 ONE-PART EPOXY GLUE

One-part epoxy glue, such as E-6000, does not need mixing as it is ready to use out of the tube. It gives a strong, flexible bond that won't become brittle and can even be used on fabric. Self-leveling, it adheres in five to ten minutes, and hardens to a clear, waterproof finish in 24 hours. You have about ten minutes to position and reposition whatever you are gluing. The only downside is that it has a strong smell so you will need to work with good ventilation.

4 SEALANTS

Sealants are available in spray form or in a bottle to paint on with a brush.

Decorative components

Decorative items such as beads, shells, and flowers are at the heart of the jewelry-making projects in this book. I have used both ready-made, store-bought items and repurposed, "found" objects (see page 21).

1 BEADS

A plethora of beads is available in every conceivable color, size, and type. Whether you are a fan of sparkly crystals, acrylic, lucite, wooden, semi-precious, pearl, or glass beads, there is bound to be something to take your fancy. Beads come in every color of the rainbow and range in size from tiny seed beads and spacers up to large focal beads.

In this book I have used a wide variety of beads; I will mention just a few examples here, as this is a topic for a whole book in itself.

Semi-precious beads are among my favorites. The colors of the chalcedony and rose quartz used in the Bee and aquilegia necklace (see pages 74–77) are really pretty. Perhaps my most favorite beads are the semi-precious labradorite stones used in the Storm clouds necklace (see pages 88–93).

I am also a fan of Czech glass beads, especially the flower and leaf shapes as used in the Forsythia brooch (see pages 158–161) and the Fruits and berries lariat (see pages 120–123).

2 CABOCHONS

Cabochons are flat-backed beads with no hole—for example, the moonstones used on the Forget-me-not necklace (see pages 64–67).

Some of the bead shapes I used include briolettes; pear-shaped ones with the holes at the top (used for the raindrops on the Forsythia brooch); ovals, rounds, rectangles, and saucers (used in the Dragonfly woods necklace, see pages 82–87).

3 ACRYLIC FLOWERS

Lightweight and inexpensive acrylic flowers can be accurate portrayals of actual flowers or more generic, but all are pretty and add a splash of color to your designs.

4 STAMPINGS

Metal stampings or charms make great focal points for your projects. They come in many different plated finishes and practically any design you can think of.

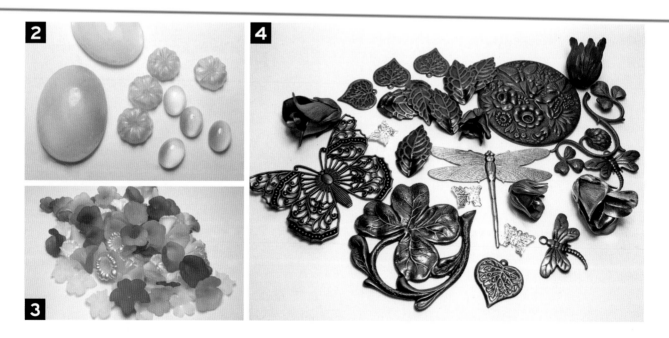

Recycled, vintage, and found materials

Terms such as "recycled," "upcycled," and "repurposed" are often used interchangeably, but they all basically involve bringing a new lease of life to an old object. In jewelry-making this might involve harvesting pretty, old, or unusual beads from a broken necklace to incorporate into a brand-new design, or simply mending an item to restore it to its former glory.

Found items are bits and pieces you could add to a design that might not normally be associated with jewelry-making; for example, hardware store nuts, bolts, and washers, or objects that are literally "found," such as shells, sea glass, feathers, pebbles, and other salvaged treasures.

SOURCING FOUND MATERIALS

Thrift stores, yard sales, online auctions, and "freecycling" sites are great places to find old items of jewelry that are no longer of any use in their present state, whether they are dirty or broken or have missing parts. Sometimes, even if just an unusual clasp or a few pretty beads can be rescued from a piece of jewelry it can be worth getting.

USING FOUND MATERIALS

If an item can be repaired or renovated—for example, if missing stones or a broken clasp can be replaced—then this can easily be done.

If something is damaged you can integrate it in whole or in part into a new design with a clear conscience. Just try to ensure that you aren't taking an heirloom apart to use in a design that will actually lessen its value. Do some research online if you are not sure; there is a wealth of experience and knowledge available.

Always check your buys for hallmarks or maker's marks before you dismantle them, as sometimes even broken pieces have value to collectors. Otherwise, enjoy plundering for beads and other components that aren't widely available and turn them into truly unique creations!

INSPIRATION AND PLANNING

Inspiration comes in many shapes and forms. My inspiration for this book came from photographs that I took of the changing seasons and the ways I found to replicate these subjects in jewelry, in abstract form using colors or textures, or working more realistically and using representative flowers, for example.

Using photography

I am no professional photographer; I am more concerned about getting the shot as you see it than becoming involved in settings, focal distances, and aperture. Sometimes breaking photographic rules yields effective pictures, while enthusiasm or good timing can compensate for lack of technical knowledge.

Obviously, you will want to use the correct settings for the type of picture required. Using a macro setting, if your camera has one, for close-ups, and using the appropriate white balance setting for daylight or artificial light will help cut down any editing time later.

Use the automatic setting on your camera if you are unsure about the more complicated options. Do take lots of pictures—it is a great shame to take only one and later discover that it is blurred.

Sketching ideas

Some people like to sketch their ideas before starting to make a project. Writing this book has been an exercise in forward planning for me, as I belong to the camp of designers for whom time spent sketching an idea could be better spent actually making something. My sketches therefore tend to be perfunctory scribbles rather than detailed designs.

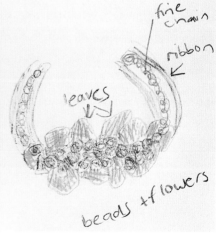

Working intuitively

Sometimes the easiest way to plan a project is simply to gather the beads that you envisage being part of your creation and working intuitively without a plan, just making up the design as you go and bringing the idea in your imagination to life.

Measuring and counting are not my forte, but I have included the quantities and sizes of beads required for each piece in this book so that you can recreate them exactly. If you can't source a specific item, use whatever you wish instead. Everything is interchangeable: Substitute different types and sizes of beads; use an alternative color scheme; use materials you already have; use vintage beads; reuse or repurpose ones from a thrift store, yard sale, or whatever you have to hand—just have fun and enjoy the process!

Physical planning

My idea of planning is to pile up the beads in a way I hope will resemble the finished project—sometimes haphazardly and usually involving many more beads than I end up with in the final piece. I start off with an exuberant and extravagant vision that (usually) ends up with something more wearable. Sometimes less is more but at other times more is better, and "everything but the kitchen sink" goes into a design. I then like to take a photograph of that random pile of beads and see how this evolves into an actual piece of jewelry.

23

WRAPPED LOOPS AND CONNECTORS

The wrapped loop is a simple way to form a connector loop on a wire length or headpin. A loop is very secure and cannot be pulled open—the only way to remove it is to cut it off. Once you are familiar with the basic technique, you can use wrapped loops to make your own beaded chain lengths or connectors.

How to make wrapped loops

1 Thread a headpin or wire through your chosen bead or beads. Using chain-nose pliers, make a right-angle bend in the headpin about ⅛in (3mm) above where you want the loop to be placed.

2 Using round-nose pliers, roll the wire back onto itself around one of the round jaws.

3 Holding the wire tail, pull it all the way around the pliers' jaw until it crosses underneath, making a loop.

4 Hold the loop in chain-nose or flat-nose pliers and, using bent-nose pliers in the other hand, pull the wire tail around the wire or headpin. Make two and a half turns.

5 Cut off the excess wire using wire cutters. Get as near to the wraps as you can to leave just a tiny amount of wire protruding.

6 Using chain-nose pliers, pinch the wire end against the wraps so that it lies flat.

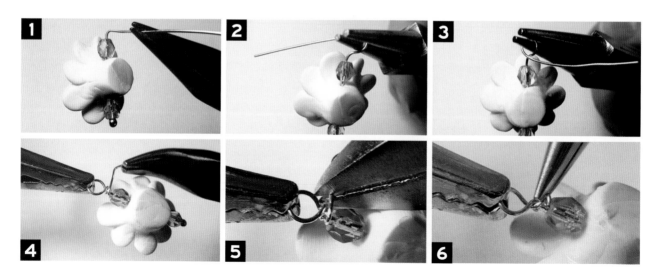

Making double-end connectors and beaded chain lengths

1 Using chain-nose pliers, start by making a right-angle bend in a 3in (75mm) length of wire. If your beads are tiny or very large, alter the length accordingly. Use round-nose pliers to make a loop.

2 Using bent-nose pliers, wrap the wire tail around to form coils, as in the basic wrapped loop technique. Add your chosen bead and then, approximately ⅛in (3mm) away from the bead, make a right-angle bend as before.

3 Using round-nose pliers, make a loop and complete the wrapped loop. You now have a bead with a loop at each end to use as a connector.

4 To start a chain and connect the looped bead without using a jumpring, slide the loop before wrapping directly onto a completed wrapped loop. You may need to pull it slightly apart first.

5 Hold the loop between chain-nose pliers and, using bent-nose pliers, wrap the wire tail into the small space you left next to the bead. Finish by cutting and tucking in the wire end.

6 Continue to add as many bead connectors attached together as you wish. You can also attach directly to chain links; this is useful if they are soldered links that cannot be opened.

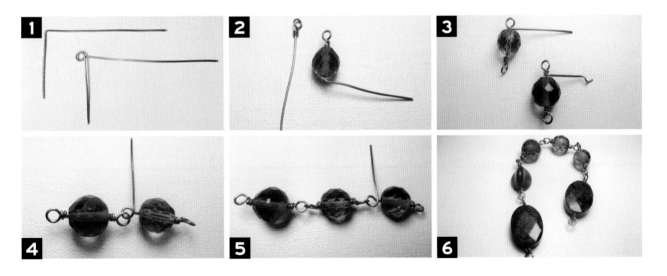

HOOK AND EYE CLASPS

Sometimes you just cannot find the clasp that you want, in either the size or the color. Making your own hook and eye clasp is easy; although the process looks as if it requires many steps, it is actually quite straightforward, and you will soon be making your own versions in all colors and sizes.

How to make the eye

1 Cut a 6in (150mm) length of wire. Fold in half around the larger part of the jaw of a pair of round-nose pliers and bring the wire ends back to make an O-shape.

2 Cut one wire ¼in (6mm) away from the loop and make a right-angle bend in the other longer wire at this point.

3 Make a smaller loop using round-nose pliers and then make several wraps around the two wires until you reach back to the first loop.

4 Cut the wire using wire cutters and trim and tuck wire end in with chain-nose pliers. The eye part is now complete.

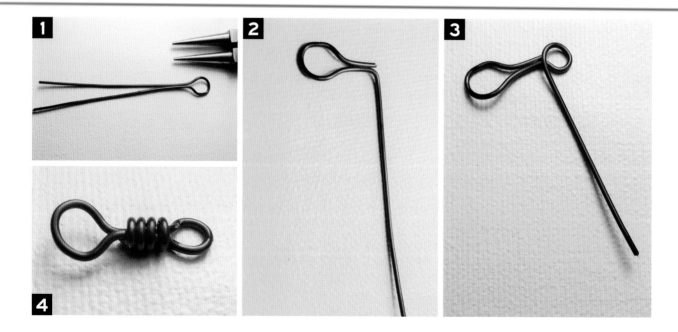

How to make the hook

1 Cut a 6in (150mm) length of wire and straighten it by running it through the jaws of a pair of nylon jaw pliers. 2in (50mm) from the end, make a bend using round-nose pliers. Bend the wire right over until it forms a U-shape and squeeze the wire together.

2 Using the smallest diameter jaw (tip) of a pair of round-nose pliers, bend the U-shaped end over to make a small loop.

3 Turning the small loop end away from you and using the largest diameter of the jaw of the round-nose pliers (nearest the plier joints), make a large loop about ¼in (6mm) below the small loop.

4 At the point where the shorter wire ends, make a right-angle bend in the longer wire using chain-nose pliers.

5 With round-nose pliers, make a loop and fold the wire back on itself to leave a tail.

6 Wrap the tail around, enclosing the short wire inside the loop and wrap several times. Cut any excess wire using wire cutters and tuck in the wire end using chain-nose pliers. The hook section of the clasp is now complete, and can be attached to the eye.

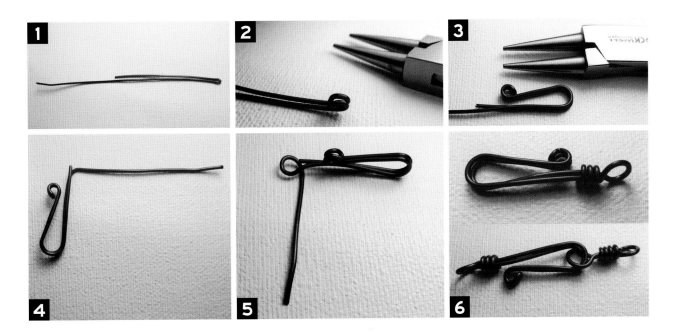

CRIMPS

Crimps are small, hollow, round, or tube-shaped metal findings that are used mainly to fasten beading wire to form a connector, for example, on the ends of a necklace or bracelet. Crimp beads come in various sizes, colors, and metals. Try not to overwork them as they can crumble and break. Crimp covers are curved beads that can be closed over the crimp for a neater appearance.

How to secure a crimp

You will need crimp pliers for this technique; chain-nose pliers can be used as well, although they do not have the shaped sections to mold the crimp bead.

1 Cut your length of beading wire using wire cutters. Use a generous amount of wire in case of mishap. If it is exactly the required length and you need to cut the crimp off then it will be too short to finish your piece. Thread the clasp loop onto the wire and then a crimp bead. Pass the wire tail through the crimp bead.

2 Using the inner, shaped part of the crimp pliers, firmly squeeze the crimp bead. It will separate the two wires and each will be in a tunnel with a flat section between.

3 Press the crimp bead with the outer, round section of the crimp pliers. Turn the crimp so that it is squashed together and rounded off. Check to see whether it will slide up and down the wire—it should not move at all. This is important: You do not want it to slip off and not hold securely.

4 Hold the crimp bead cover in chain-nose pliers with the open side upward. You may need to open the cover out slightly using pliers.

5 Slide the crimp bead and wire into the crimp cover and press steadily with the pliers until the crimp cover closes around the crimp bead. Do not squeeze too hard as it will distort the crimp cover shape.

6 You can now add beads. Slide the wire tail through several consecutive bead holes and then trim with wire cutters. Take care not to cut the main wire as you do this.

Repeat once all beads are threaded at the other end. Trim excess wire only when you are certain the crimp is secure.

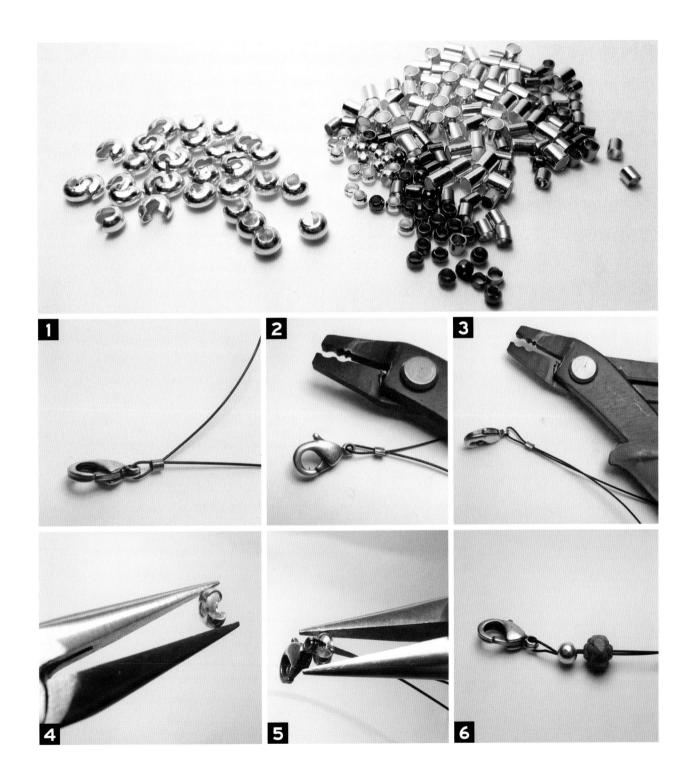

29

SHRINK PLASTIC

You can cut shrink plastic into any shape; color it, paint it, print on it, or stamp onto it with ink. Shrink plastic comes in many colors and finishes. It becomes a hard plastic shape that is 50 percent of its original size when heated with a heat gun or baked in a stove. Here I have made the components that feature in the Butterflies and thistles tiara (see pages 100–104). Each brand of heat-shrink plastic may have slightly different instructions, so follow those.

How to use shrink plastic

1 Draw your designs using a fine permanent marker pen, or use a rubber stamp and permanent ink to stamp your design onto the shrink plastic sheet.

2 Make holes using a hole punch so that you can insert thread wire through your shapes. Then color in your designs using pencils.

3 Cut out neatly using sharp scissors. Try to slide the scissors; be careful not to accidentally snip corners or small details off as the blades can slip easily and cut the brittle plastic sheet.

4 Place the cut-out shape on a heatproof block and hold in place using tweezers. Do not hold using the hole as it will distort during heating.

5 Heat using a heat gun and keep it moving over the plastic. The plastic will wriggle and fold alarmingly but will flatten out again once fully shrunk.

6 Press over the design with a folded piece of paper to flatten it. Take care, as it will still be hot. The shapes are ready to use once cooled.

MOLDS AND CASTS

Making your own molds gives you the versatility to recreate small objects using epoxy clay, polymer clay, or resin. Silicone putty is a two-part non-toxic substance that, once mixed, can be used to make a permanent impression of shells, buttons, or anything durable enough to withstand being pressed into the putty.

How to make a silicone mold

1 Measure one part each of silicone putty in equal amounts. It usually comes in two different colors, one per pot. You can roll it into a ball to judge the quantity or use a measuring scoop. Wear gloves to ensure that you don't accidentally contaminate the pots by transferring putty from one pot to another.

2 Using your hands, thoroughly mix together the two colors of putty until it is one even color. Spend no longer than 30 seconds mixing it; once mixed, you have only about five minutes of working time before the putty starts to cure.

3 Roll the mixed putty into a ball and then flatten it on a non-stick surface. Press the object firmly into the putty. Do not push it too far in or the back wall of the mold will be too thin. Tuck the putty snugly against the side of the object. Allow it to cure for 20 minutes.

4 Test the mold with your fingernail. If it leaves an indentation, wait a few more minutes. Gently flex the mold from behind so that the object pops out. The mold is now ready to use. Remove any debris left in the mold or it will be replicated every time you use it.

The plastic inner wrapper of a cereal box makes a great disposable nonstick surface to work on. Make sure you wash it thoroughly before use.

33

How to make clay casts

Epoxy clay, such as Apoxie Sculpt, is a two-part resin "clay" that does not require baking. It remains pliable for two to three hours after mixing and sets hard after 24 hours.

1 Measure out two equal amounts of parts A and B, use a measuring scoop or judging by eye. Wear gloves for this stage. Rolling into balls helps to judge the quantity. Again, do not cross-contaminate the two tubs.

2 Still wearing gloves, mix the two parts together thoroughly. Epoxy clay is sticky once mixed and loves you, your gloves, and any surface. If it is unmanageably sticky, leave it for 30 minutes to set slightly, or place it in the fridge to chill, but bear in mind that this reduces the working time. Try putting a small amount of petroleum jelly on your gloves, or have a small pot of cold water to dip your fingers into.

3 Press small amounts of epoxy clay into the mold. It saves on the amount of sanding down required later if there is less overhang from the top of the mold. You can also use a small amount of water on your gloves to smooth the epoxy clay into the mold. Make sure you press it in firmly to ensure that all the details are captured.

If making multiples from one mold, then flex the mold carefully to remove the epoxy clay and place it gently on waxed paper while you repeat the molding process. If you are making just one item that does not need a hole then leave it to dry in the mold for 24 hours for a perfect copy.

4 Make hanging holes at this stage with a cocktail stick, being careful to not distort the molded shape. Wire loops can also be added now for attachments. Make a wrapped loop and leave a small tail, then make a kink in the wire with pliers so it cannot be pulled out once dry.

5 When totally set, after 24 hours, sand down any excess and smooth around the holes. This is a messy job as the dust is powdery. Wear appropriate safety equipment including goggles and a mask to avoid inhaling the dust. You can use a sanding block, an emery board, or regular sandpaper to do this.

6 Rinse under the tap or wipe the excess dust from the molded pieces. They can be painted now as required. Use a couple of coats for coverage and seal afterward. Once the paint and sealer has dried completely, the charms are ready to use. Attach to bracelets or necklaces using jumprings or thread thong or cord through the holes. They are lightweight enough to be used in earrings.

35

RESIN

Two-part resin is very versatile, and modern types will not yellow with age. All manner of items can be included into the resin, such as paper, charms, beads, buttons, watch parts, pressed flowers, mica powder or eyeshadow, glitter, leaves, and segments of photographs. The only rule is that the items to be set must be completely dry. Any moisture will prevent the resin from setting properly, or it may become cloudy.

How to use resin

Resin can be used as a glaze coating, sanded, drilled, layered, or molded; you can even mix oil paint into it. For the purpose of this book I will just cover how to set photograph segments into bezels, as used, for example, in the Sunset bracelet (see pages 108–11). Always make extras if you have enough spare components to cover any eventuality. It is tricky to mix tiny amounts of resin—the minimum I would mix is ½oz/15g (that is, ¼oz/7g of both hardener and resin)—therefore it makes sense to work in batches as surplus bezels can be used on other projects.

1 Wear latex or nitrile disposable gloves. Resin is very sticky and extremely difficult to remove. Also use a table protector. Leave any spills on there to dry and they will peel off.

You will need two measuring cups, with graduations marked on the side. My preferred amount to mix is ½oz/15g, so that requires ¼oz/7g of each of the two parts, the resin and the hardener. Measure carefully: If you have too much hardener it will still set, but if you have too much resin you will have a sticky mess that never hardens.

2 Add the runnier of the two parts into the other measuring cup once you have poured the desired amount.

3 Fold the two parts together using a wooden stick such as a popsicle stick. Mix thoroughly. Stirring too briskly makes lots of bubbles, although these will dissipate if you leave the mixture to stand for a few moments. Any bubbles remaining after pouring can be popped with a cocktail stick. Your resin is now ready to use in your projects. Working time is approximately 45 minutes to one hour.

Resin will harden in approximately six hours and be fully cured in 24 hours.

4 These are the resin-filled bezels from the Sunset bracelet project (see pages 108–11) before making a "dome" on the flat surface. They have been allowed to dry for 24 hours. You can also add resin in layers to include items within the resin, working in thin layers and allowing it to dry before adding the next.

5 The resin is self-doming: If you carefully add it drop by drop using a wooden popsicle stick it will stay higher in the center, providing you have it on a level surface. Work slowly to avoid messy overspills, although these can be snipped off once the resin is dry.

6 Cover drying items with a bowl or plastic cover to prevent dust settling into the resin surface.

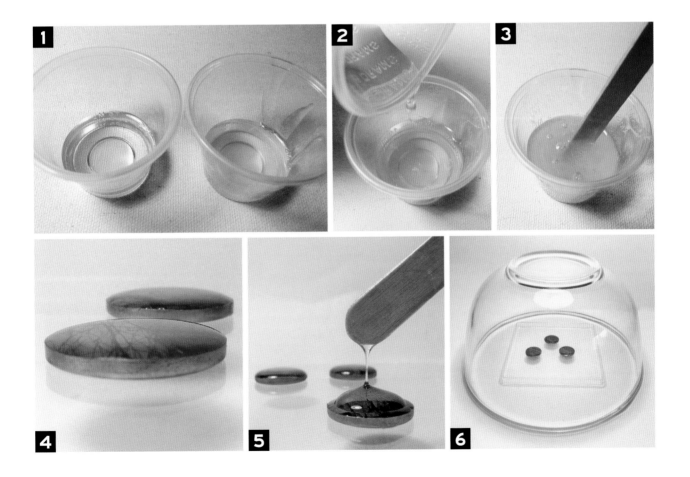

DYE OXIDE PAINTS

Water-based dye oxide paints can be used to color metal (such as stampings) and can also be used over metal-coating paints. You will need a glass or metal dish to put the dye oxide into. Pour any excess back into the bottle once it has cooled and remember to wash it thoroughly between colors.

How to color metal using dye oxide paints

1 Set up your work area with a heatproof base cloth (the type plumbers use to protect pipes while soldering) and a heatproof block (the sort you would use with a blow torch). Both of these items become hot during use and retain heat for some time. An absorbent cloth underneath is useful for any spills or splashes.

2 Wash the stampings thoroughly in hot water and detergent. Leave to dry. Grease and dirt from fingerprints or the factory will repel colors, so try not to handle the items using your ungloved fingers after this.

3 Pour a little of the chosen color of dye oxide into the dish. I used fall shades for these leaves. Place a leaf stamping onto the soldering block and, using a heat gun, heat gently and steadily. Do not heat until it is red hot, as some stampings will melt or distort. Use heatproof tweezers to pick the piece up—it helps if you slide it to hang over the edge of the block a little—and drop it into the dye oxide.

4 Allow the leaf to cool slightly in the dye oxide and then, using tweezers, remove it and place it back on the block and heat again until the dye oxide has dried. You should see a layer of color starting to form. Turn the leaf and make sure the reverse side is dry.

5 Heat the leaf again and drop it back into the dye oxide. Remove and heat again to set the color. Repeat these steps until the color has reached the intensity you want. Some colors are more transparent than others and require more layers. Pour any excess dye oxide back into the bottle once it has cooled.

6 Seal the leaves using a spray or brush-on sealant, otherwise the color will scratch off and not be permanent.

When using a heat gun the metal becomes hot; the dye oxide can spit while in the pot when heated objects are placed in it and also during heating to set it. Wear goggles and gloves and protect surfaces from heat and staining. Work in a well-ventilated area—sometimes metals can smell strongly once heated. Wash off any splashes of dye oxide from your skin immediately as it will stain.

SPRING INSPIRATIONS

Spring heralds the start of lengthening days and increasing warm sunshine. This is a time of rebirth and renewal, when flowers burst into life, trees blossom and leaves unfurl, and swathes of bluebells carpet verdant woodlands.

Nodding heads of golden daffodils, carpets of bluebells in green woodlands, magnolias unfurling flowers like the sails on a galleon, shocking pink bleeding hearts, and trees laden with sugar-pink blossom.

The spring projects are inspired by the season's predominant flowers. From the delicate blue forget-me-not necklace to the candy pink blossom bracelet, you'll find plenty of projects to choose from to brighten up your wardrobe.

43

DAFFODIL NECKLACE

A host of golden daffodils nodding in a gentle breeze is a sure sign that spring has arrived at last. On this delicate necklace, muted jonquil and pale green shades of Czech glass beads accompany a cluster of acrylic flowers on a beaded chain.

- 2 x two-part acrylic daffodils, 25mm (or substitute separate flower and 10mm bell flower for center)
- 6 x Czech glass five-petal green/beige flowers, 6 x 9mm
- 6 x Czech glass round jonquils, 5mm
- 2 x Czech glass polished amber rectangles, 12 x 9mm
- 4 x Czech glass transparent jonquil flowers, 6 x 6mm
- 2 x Czech glass round jonquils, 2mm
- 6 x Czech glass mixed greens, 4mm
- 9 x acrylic bell flowers in yellow and pale green, 10mm
- 20in (500mm) length of rolo chain, 4mm diameter
- 2in (50mm) length of scroll chain, 2 x 5mm
- Headpins, 50mm
- 9 x ball-end headpins, 50mm
- 1 x trigger clasp

- Round-nose pliers
- Bent-nose pliers
- Wire cutters
- Chain-nose pliers

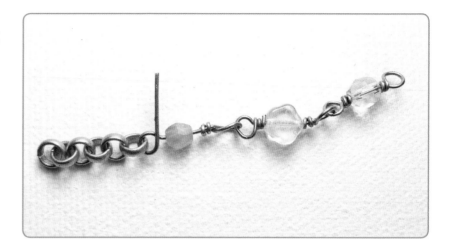

1 Begin the beaded chain section by making a wrapped looped bead connector (see page 25). Attach the first loop to the previous bead as you go along. Continue to add wrapped loop bead connectors and include two sections of six links of rolo chain.

2 Starting with a ball-end 50mm headpin, add a 2mm jonquil, a flower center, flower petals, and a Czech glass green/beige flower. Make a wrapped loop to secure. Repeat for a second flower.

Beaded chain can be time-consuming to make. To speed up the process, you can attach the wrapped loop links together using jumprings.

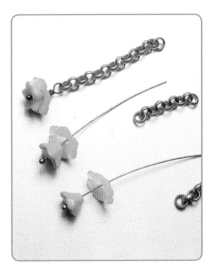

3 Connect the longer chain pieces onto the last wrapped loop of the beaded sections. Add the trigger clasp. On a small section of thin scroll chain, add a bead drop and attach it using a jumpring.

4 Cut three lengths of rolo chain in staggered lengths of 6, 9, and 12 links long. Using ball-end headpins, make three bead dangles using the acrylic flowers and centers to construct daffodils and then add a bead dangle on the end of each section of chain.

5 Fasten the large daffodils and the three chain dangles along with the beaded chain ends onto a jumpring to attach together.

6 Make four more beaded dangle flowers on 50mm headpins and add to the chain with jumprings.

PINK BLOSSOM BRACELET

Heavily laden trees burst with pink flowers like delicious confectionery, and every breeze produces a shower of confetti-like petals. Preserve the short-lived beauty of this time under a layer of icy-clear resin in this simple-to-make bracelet.

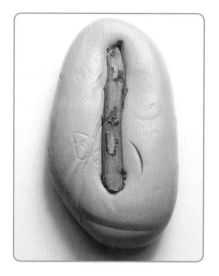

1 Make a silicone mold of a short piece of twig (see pages 32–33). Pick a twig that has some texture rather than using a smooth section. Mold six twig pieces from two-part resin clay.

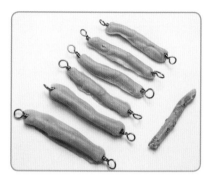

2 Add wire loops to each end while still soft. Allow to dry, then sand down any excess.

3 Apply metal paint using a brush. Do two coats and let dry. Seal and leave to dry.

4 Make a wrapped loop (see page 24) for three lots of tiny yellow and white beads on a length of US 20-gauge (SWG 21, 0.8mm) wire. Wrap again to hold the beads snugly in position. These form the stamens.

6 Shape the wire ends so that they will tuck into the hollow back of the branch stamping.

5 Add eight shell beads onto ball-end headpins. Bunch them together with the stamens in the center. When you are happy with the arrangement, wrap US 24-gauge (SWG 25, 0.5mm) wire tightly around the stems to secure.

If you make a necklace long enough then it does not require a clasp—it will go over your head.

7 Mix a small amount of two-part epoxy glue on a scrap piece of card using a cocktail stick as a stirrer. Apply glue to a branch stamping and then firmly clip into place to dry. This type of glue sets in about 10 minutes.

8 Make wrapped loops of beads and attach them directly to the twigs you made. You could use jumprings to attach if preferred.

9 Fasten all sections together and add a length of chain. Add bead dangles in clusters to each join between the twigs and wrapped bead sections.

BLEEDING HEART BRACELET

These dainty little heart-shaped flowers, with their striking bright pink colors, look so pretty strung along the branches of this shrub in spring. I wanted to make a really "pretty-in-pink" bracelet, so chose wire, beads, and chain all in coordinating shades.

YOU WILL NEED

- 7 x fuchsia acrylic heart beads, 14mm
- 24 x fuchsia Czech glass heart beads, 6mm
- 38 x fuchsia acrylic bicone crystal beads, 4mm
- 7in (175mm) length of flat chain, plus some links for jumprings
- US 18-gauge (SWG 19, 1mm) magenta-colored wire (to make the hook and eye clasp)
- US 20-gauge (SWG 21, 0.8mm) magenta-colored wire

- Round-nose pliers
- Wire cutters
- Chain-nose pliers
- Bent-nose pliers

1 Cut the chain to bracelet length using wire cutters, or simply undo the links using bent-nose and chain-nose pliers. My chain was 7in (175mm) long; it could be cut to any length to suit, but remember that the clasp will add on a few inches (depending how big you make it) and that you need some slack to be able to fasten it.

2 Using round-nose pliers and 3in (75mm) sections of US 20-gauge (SWG 21, 0.8mm) wire, make a tiny loop using the smallest part of the pliers' jaw to make an eyepin. Repeat to make an eyepin for each dangle.

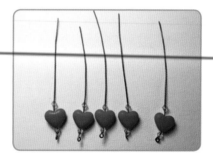

3 On your eyepins, thread on a 4mm bicone crystal, then a 14mm acrylic heart, then another 4mm bicone crystal. Repeat for each of the seven acrylic hearts. Make these into wrapped loop dangles (see page 24).

A word about wire thickness: to make a sturdy clasp, US 18-gauge (SWG 19, 1mm) wire is most suitable. However, you can use thinner gauges if you hammer the wire loops on a steel block after forming them—don't hammer the wrapped loopy parts though, as you will distort them.

4 Now make wrapped loops with all 24 of the 6mm hearts. Add a 4mm bicone crystal onto each eyepin, then a 6mm heart, and make wrapped loop dangles as before.

5 Using chain link to act as jumprings, attach each wrapped loop dangle to the chain. Find the center point first and add a 14mm acrylic heart here, then add equal numbers of dangles to either side.

6 Make the hook and eye clasp from US 18-gauge (SWG 19, 1mm) wire (see pages 26–27), and add to each end of the chain using chain links as jumprings.

Sometimes it is tricky to find the exact color of eyepin you require. Making your own is easy, and using chain links from colored chain is a great way to match up jumprings if you are working with a less common color.

BLUEBELL BRACELET

On this bracelet, I wanted to try to capture the sheer exuberance of springtime woods carpeted with bluebells and loaded with flowers and greenery. A silk ribbon slotted through the chain adds a pretty touch to an abundance of blue flowers.

- 9 x polymer clay bluebells (I used ones by Elise Canning; see page 166), 16mm
- 4 x green acrylic tulip beads, 12 x 12mm
- 7 x blue acrylic tulip beads, 12 x 12mm
- 5 x acrylic dogwood flowers, 13mm
- 3 x polymer clay mini bluebell flowers (I used ones by Elise Canning; see page 166), 10mm
- 10 x acrylic baby's breath flowers, 6mm
- 9 x acrylic camellia flowers, 14mm

- 12 x frosted green leaves, 21 x 23mm
- Indian glass bead mix in blue (3 x large teardrops and 7 x centers on leaves); teardrops 12mm, centers 8mm
- 14 x periwinkle round glass beads, 8mm
- 29 x green round glass frosted beads, 6mm
- 12 x seed beads (on reverse of leaves)
- 6 x baby bell blueberry glass flower beads, 6mm
- 2 x brass filigree rectangles, 30 x 13mm

- 18in (460mm) length of raw brass rolo chain, 4mm diameter
- 6in (150mm) length of natural brass textured book chain
- 12in (305mm) length of lilac-mix silk ribbon
- Brass headpins, 50mm
- Bronze jumprings, 5mm
- 1 x lobster clasp
- Super glue (to secure ribbon knot)

- Wire cutters
- Chain-nose pliers
- Bent-nose pliers
- Chain Sta grips

1 Using wire cutters or opening links, cut all chain lengths to size; note that the clasp will add 2.5cm. Lay out the lengths between the filigree rectangles. Using 5mm jumprings, attach the chains at both ends to the filigree. Fasten short lengths of chain to the outer edge of the filigree; attach a lobster clasp at one end and a series of 5mm jumprings linked together at the other end.

2 Put all beads and flowers onto headpins. Add seed beads to the back of the leaves where holes are large enough for the headpin to pass through.

3 Make all beads into wrapped loop dangles (see page 24). Work in batches—work all the same step on each headpin to speed up this process.

4 Thread the silk ribbon through the slots on the book chain along the whole length of it. Wrap several times at each end and tie a bow. Dab super glue on the knot so the bow stays tied and apply a little on the cut ends to prevent the ribbon from fraying.

If you don't feel confident enough to construct your own bracelet base, using a bought charm bracelet blank is ideal; you can then just concentrate on adorning it with beads.

5 Clamp the rolo chain section on one side into the Chain Sta grips. This keeps the chain from twisting and holds it so you have both hands free. Divide the wrapped loop dangles roughly in half. Using chain-nose and bent-nose pliers and 5mm jumprings, add half the dangles to the chain. Add them symmetrically or randomly as you please.

6 Turn the bracelet around so the side with no dangles is in the Chain Sta, and add the remainder of the dangles using 5mm jumprings to this side. Add a blueberry bell bead to the end of the clasp chain.

FORGET-ME-NOT NECKLACE

This necklace, with its cluster of handmade polymer flowers and beads in matching colors, combined with dreamy blue glass moonstones, captures the feel of a warm spring day. I used a mix of flower shapes and beads, both new and vintage.

8 Make simple matching earrings by gluing the small cabs into the setting. Add a flower drop with a 4mm jumpring and attach to an earring wire.

7 Fasten the beaded links and chain sections together using jumprings and add the drops hanging from one larger jumpring—three on each ring. Add a jumpring to each end of chain and secure to the flower cluster pendant. Add a clasp of your choice to the other chain ends.

US 24-gauge (SWG 25, 0.5mm) and all thinner-gauge wires may become brittle after repeatedly threading backward and forward several times. If the wire kinks, smooth it out with your fingers—do not tug or it may snap.

SUMMER INSPIRATIONS

The hazy, long, hot days of summer are characterized by fragrant plants in full bloom, and profuse and lavish gardens humming with bees. Brightly colored butterflies flit through lush, flower-filled meadows, while rising heat sparks sudden summer storms.

Pendulous aquilegias tremble with bees; abundant buttercups and daisies dot verdant lawns. In the woods a darting dragonfly flashes in the dappled light. Heat sparks a storm with dark, foreboding clouds. Roses trail lazily over the garden trellis and butterflies flutter among thorny thistles.

Summer projects are bright and colorful, from the cheerful buttercups and daisies bracelet, to a fun butterfly tiara. Colors are hot and bold, and the jewelry is eye-catching.

BEE AND AQUILEGIA NECKLACE

In the drifting sunlight on a summer's afternoon, a bee languidly buzzes from one aquilegia flower to another. For this necklace, I chose dreamy shades of lilac, pink, and purple semi-precious stones, and clusters of acrylic flowers.

YOU WILL NEED

- 1 x polymer clay pink aquilegia flower, 30mm
- 2 x rose quartz double-carved roses, 14mm
- 5 x lilac chalcedony ovals, 10 x 8mm
- 2 x purple faceted chalcedony ovals, 18 x 13mm
- 10 x green faceted Czech glass oval beads, 6mm
- 6 x amethyst fluted glass beads, 9mm
- 24 x lilac and pink acrylic bell flowers, 10mm
- 24 x bronze spacer beads, 4mm
- 24 x seed beads, 2mm

- 1 x brass bee stamping, 26 x 33mm
- 2 x brass bee three-ring connectors, 20 x 17mm
- Length of copper ox ladder chain
- US 20-gauge (SWG 21, 0.8mm) wire
- Jumprings, 5mm
- Ball-end headpins
- Oval jumprings
- 1 x toggle clasp

- Wire cutters
- Round-nose pliers
- Bent-nose pliers
- Chain-nose pliers

2 Using the larger purple chalcedony ovals and the rose quartz roses with a green crystal on each side and 3in (75mm) lengths of US 20-gauge (SWG 21, 0.8mm) wire, make connectors with a wrapped loop at each end (see page 25). If the bee stamping has no hole, then punch one using a hole punch. Turn the polymer clay aquilegia flower into a connector by threading US 20-gauge (SWG 21, 0.8mm) wire through the holes and making a wrapped loop at each side.

1 Make up the 24 acrylic flower and smaller chalcedony lilac ovals into wrapped loop dangles on the ball-end headpins using all three types of pliers and wire cutters (see page 24). Add seed beads between the ball-end headpins and the flowers if the bead holes are larger than the headpins. Finish with a bronze spacer bead. Also make some dangles with the amethyst fluted beads and green glass beads.

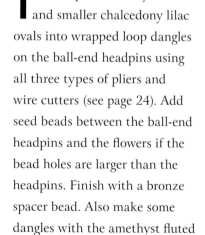

If the bead holes are larger than the ends on headpins, simply add a seed bead to stop the headpin passing through the bead hole.

3 On a short length of chain, add wrapped loop dangles to alternate links using 5mm jumprings. This is the section that will hang behind the bee stamping.

4 Add the toggle clasp and toggle to each end of the chain lengths using 5mm jumprings and a larger oval jumpring for the toggle part. Using 5mm jumprings, fasten the connector sections together and the three-ring bee connectors to construct the main body of the necklace.

5 With an oval jumpring, attach the wrapped loop connector polymer clay aquilegia flower, bee stamping, chain dangle, and bead connector together.

6 Make clusters of flower dangles by adding five flowers and bead wrapped loop dangles onto a 5mm jumpring, then fasten the jumpring to the loops along the necklace length and to the connector loop on the bee wings.

BUTTERCUPS AND DAISIES BRACELET

Fresh-as-a-daisy swirly green vintage plastic beads complement polymer clay buttercups and daisies on this summery-looking bracelet. These elements combine with wonderful 1950s ceramic Japanese Aojiso leaves to give a snapshot of a sunny day.

- 5 x polymer clay daisies (I used ones by Elise Canning; see page 166), 20mm
- 6 x polymer clay buttercups (I used ones by Elise Canning; see page 166), 18mm
- 8 x vintage plastic swirly green beads (6 large, 2 small), 14mm and 10mm
- 10 x Chrysolite celsian melon-shaped Czech glass beads, 8mm

- 10 x green bicone crystal beads, 4mm
- 20 x Czech glass green mix rondelles, 4 x 6mm
- 2 x 1950s Japanese ceramic Aojiso leaves, 25 x 30mm
- 7in (175mm) length of silver-plated chain
- Ball-end headpins, 50mm
- Silver jumprings, 4mm
- 2 x 10mm silver jumprings (for leaves)

- 1 x brass leaf toggle clasp (I used one from Trinity)
- 1 x brass leaf toggle bar (I used one from Trinity brass)

- Round-nose pliers
- Bent-nose pliers
- Wire cutters
- Chain-nose pliers
- Chain Sta grips

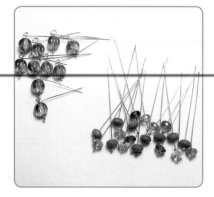

1 Using 4mm jumprings, attach the clasp toggle and bar to each end of the chain length.

2 Using the wrapped loop technique (see page 24), turn all flowers and beads into bead dangles. Add a 4mm bicone to either side of the polymer clay daisies on the headpin to make constructing the wire loop easier.

3 Once all the beads and flowers are on headpins with a wrapped loop dangle, you are ready to add them onto the chain.

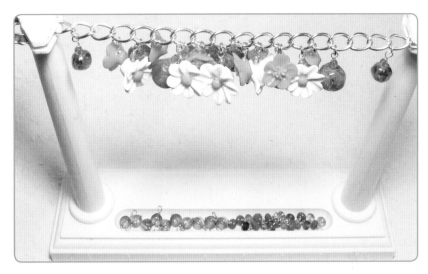

4 Affix the chain and clasp onto the Chain Sta using the clips to secure. This device holds the chain taut and stops it twisting every time you add a bead. Using 4mm jumprings, start to attach beads to the chain links. Work from the center of the chain outward.

5 Attach all the larger beads and flowers first and then fill in the spaces with the smaller beads. Hang on the same part of the chain link, either at the top or bottom edge, for a more uniform finish.

When making a large number of wrapped loop beaded dangles, it is easier to work in batches and do all the steps on each bead at the same time to avoid constantly swapping tools.

6 Using 10mm jumprings, attach the large ceramic leaves to the center of the bracelet.

DRAGONFLY
WOODS NECKLACE

This piece was inspired by my favorite place; where the reflections in the river of the lush, almost primeval, woodland are magical. Sometimes bead magic happens too—the teardrop beads were a lucky find, but could not have been a better match.

YOU WILL NEED

- 1 x photograph of woods and water scene
- Gloss sealer spray or brush-on sealant
- Glue for paper or card
- Two-part resin
- Popsicle stick
- Black acrylic paint
- Matte sealant
- 1 x brass curtain ring, 2in (50mm) diameter (or use any size and cut the photo to fit)
- 4 x teardrop peridot glass beads, 10 x 7mm

- 8 x teardrop green plastic beads (or substitute any coordinating/contrasting beads), 17 x 12mm
- 2 x bright green swirly plastic beads (or substitute any beads of your choice), 14mm
- 2 x Czech glass Picasso peridot saucer beads, 9 x 7mm
- 2 x green glass rondelles, 14mm
- 1 x round brass openwork filigree flower, 47mm
- 1 x brass dragonfly stamping, 42 x 50mm

- 4in (100mm) of bronze medium link chain
- US 20-gauge (SWG 21, 0.8mm) bronze wire
- 4 x brass Art Nouveau bird bead caps, 15 x 13mm
- 4 x brass beehive bead caps, 4mm
- 1 x toggle clasp and loop

- Scissors
- Wire cutters
- Chain-nose pliers
- Bent-nose pliers
- Flat-nose pliers

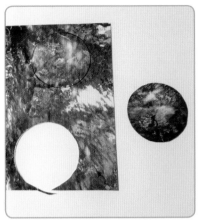

1 Using a ballpoint pen (as it leaves an indentation on the photograph), draw around the outside edge of the brass curtain ring on the part of the photo you wish to use. Spray or brush on sealer to prevent the resin bleeding into the photograph. Leave to dry and then cut out with sharp scissors.

2 Glue around the edges on the reverse of the curtain ring and firmly stick the photo to it. Make sure it is a good join or the resin will leak.

3 Following the steps on pages 36–37 (see also the steps for the Pink blossom bracelet, pages 48–51), mix the resin and add slowly to cover the photo in the curtain-ring bezel. Do not fill the resin to the brim, as you want the dragonfly to "hover" over the surface. Cover to avoid dust settling in the resin while drying and leave for at least 12 hours.

4 Paint the reverse of the bezel with black acrylic paint and allow it to dry. Seal the paint with multipurpose matte sealer and allow to dry. Position four teardrop peridot glass stones so that they will fit into the spaces on the brass filigree and then glue into place.

5 Once the glued stones are dry, glue the filigree into place over the top. Before securing, add a jumpring at the top as it is tricky to attach once glued down. Use clamps or tweezers to hold the piece firmly in place while the glue dries.

6 Dab glue on the edges of the curtain-ring bezel where the dragonfly's wings and tail will touch; firmly press into position, clamp into place, and leave to dry.

7 Using 3in (75mm) sections of US 20-gauge (SWG 21, 0.8mm) bronze wire, construct the bead connectors and make wrapped loops at each end around the 14mm plastic swirly beads (note the fabulous Art Nouveau-style birds on the bead caps). Add the beehive bead caps on either side of the bird bead caps.

8 Attach the connectors with chain links used as jumprings to each side of the dragonfly. Add beaded connectors.

You can work in layers with resin, adding inclusions (items) to give a 3D effect. Allow each layer to dry before adding the next.

9 Finish the necklace with a short section of chain and toggle clasp.

STORM CLOUDS
NECKLACE

Dark clouds gather for a summer storm, looming and ominous, and obscuring the daylight. This multi-strand necklace is heavy with semi-precious stones: beautiful labradorite with its lightning flashes within, gray druzy agate, and glass raindrop beads.

- 5 x labradorite rectangle faceted stones, 18 x 13mm
- 22 x labradorite oval faceted stones, 19 x 14mm
- 6 x labradorite rondelles, 9 x 6mm
- 30 x labradorite faceted coins, 12mm
- 37 x gray druzy quartz agate round stones, 10mm
- 26 x labradorite ovals, 7 x 9mm

- 10 x gray/white teardrop glass beads, 7mm
- 22in (560mm) length of flat medium chain in black
- 18in (460mm) length of double-link chain in black
- 21-strand beading wire
- 1 x black toggle clasp
- 2 x black two-connector ring

- Black ball-end headpins, 50mm
- Black jumprings, 6mm
- Crimps, 3mm

- Crimp pliers
- Wire cutters
- Chain-nose pliers
- Bent-nose pliers
- Flat-nose pliers

1 Fold the 18in (460mm) double-link chain in half and attach the two-connector toggle clasp parts to each end by opening chain links. Cut the chain in half at the center point and attach the connector rings to the ends, again using chain links. This forms a sturdy section for the back of the necklace.

2 Attach a generous length of 21-strand beading wire using a crimp to the connector ring. Pass the beading wire through the ring and slide a crimp along the wire. Use crimping pliers to first squash the crimp and then fold it over to secure the beading wire, leaving a tail that will thread through the bead holes.

For heavy necklaces, always use 21-strand beading wire—you do not want the strands to break!

3 Thread the first strand of beads, the labradorite rectangles and rondelles, along the wire; tuck the beading wire tail into the first few beads to hide and secure it. This will be the shortest of the strands, which gradually increase in length so that they drape nicely when worn.

4 When the first strand of beads is strung, fasten the beading wire end to the opposite connector ring by threading a crimp after the last bead, pass the beading wire around the ring and back through the crimp. Using crimping pliers, flatten and press the crimp. Test whether it slides along the wire before letting go. If it does move, then flatten and tighten more (take care because the crimps are delicate and can crumble). Only when you are satisfied that it is holding fast, cut the wire tail off after passing through several beads.

5 Measure the next strand of chain against the first row to ensure that it is slightly longer than the previous strand, remembering to allow for the jumprings to fasten it. Each subsequent strand should be slightly longer—measure them against each other as you progress.

6 Add teardrop glass beads onto ball-end headpins and make a loop as if to make wrapped loops. Thread that loop directly onto the chain links and finish making the wrapped loops to make "raindrop" dangles. If preferred, you can attach using jumprings after making the completed wrapped loop.

7 Using jumprings, attach the chain with dangles to the connector rings.

8 Add the next strand of 7 x 9mm labradorite ovals as per steps 3 and 4, making sure they will be longer than the chain-and-dangles strand.

9 Continue to add beaded strands interspersed with lengths of chain, of labradorite ovals, chain, gray druzy agate stones, chain, and labradorite ovals to finish.

ROSE CAMEO CHOKER

The scent of roses growing in my garden is the most gorgeous, summery fragrance. For this choker, I used a resin cameo, painted to look like old brass. I combined the cameo with shades of pink and tawny beads, and fastened it with sari ribbon.

8 Continue wrapping with wire and adding rose beads. When you reach the other end, wrap the wire tightly, cut any excess, and tuck in the wire end. Make a wrapped loop with the 16-gauge wire to secure. At this point you could simply add a clasp to the wire loops using jumprings.

9 Make the "eye" part of a hook and eye clasp (see pages 26–27) using US 16-gauge (SWG 18, 1.2mm) wire. As you construct it, slot the two sari ribbon ends into the larger hole and make the wrapped loop part of the eye on the end loop of the choker section. Fold the ribbons back onto themselves to make a loop and wrap tightly, using US 20-gauge (SWG 21, 0.8mm) wire to secure. Cut off any excess wire and tuck in the ends. Tie a loose knot to fasten.

BUTTERFLIES AND THISTLES TIARA

This is a fun, lighthearted, and ever so slightly over-the-top tiara with tortoiseshell butterflies and thistles twisted with green wire to create a summer meadow headpiece. I made my own butterflies and thistles from heat-shrink plastic for this project.

- Butterflies and thistles made from heat-shrink plastic (see pages 30–31); I used 7 butterflies, 6 thistle heads, and 6 thistle leaves
- 12 x green glass beads, 4mm
- US 16-gauge (SWG 18, 1.25mm) green-colored wire
- US 22-gauge (SWG 23, 0.6mm) green-colored wire
- Round object such as a tin to shape base

- Hammer and block
- Round-nose pliers
- Chain-nose pliers
- Flat-nose pliers
- Wire cutters

1 To make the tiara base, cut a 29½in (750mm) length of US 16-gauge (SWG 18, 1.25mm) wire. Bend it in half, making a loop at the bend with round-nose pliers. Holding with flat-nose pliers, twist so that the two wires wrap around each other and twist together. Make a wrapped loop (see page 24) at the other end—these loops allow the headpiece to be attached to hair using grips.

2 Shape the twisted wire around a circular object such as an old tin or box. Press against the shape to form a U-shaped base with your fingers.

To twist wire neatly for a less organic look you can use a drill bit or a pin vise.

3 Hammer lightly on a steel block to harden the wire, but take care not to mar the wire with the hammer head.

4 Thread one of the shrink plastic thistle pieces with a 15¾in (400mm) length of US 22-gauge (SWG 23, 0.6mm). Wire down through the lower hole, up the reverse, back out the top hole, and over the hole—loop and back along the reverse and then twist back on itself to form a stem.

5 Repeat the same steps along either or both wire tails to add leaves, and also for the butterfly "stems."

6 Arrange all the stems to decide the order in which they will be attached to the base. Usually the longest stems are in the center, with shorter ones graduating out to the sides.

7 Attach the upright stems to the tiara base wire by placing the wire tails on each side of the base. Wrap in opposite directions around the base to hold them in place. You can use your fingers to wrap before cutting the ends with wire cutters. Use chain-nose pliers to tuck the wire ends in on the outer edge of the base to prevent scratching when the tiara is worn.

If you are drawing a design onto the shrink plastic freehand, draw it on paper first then trace it on to the shrink plastic so you can replicate it easily and quickly.

8 Continue to attach the stems to the base, working from each side inward. Shape each stem as desired so that the leaves and butterflies curve around each other using your fingers or round-nose pliers.

9 Cut a 35½in (900mm) length of US 22-gauge (SWG 23, 0.6mm) wire and start wrapping tightly around the base wire halfway between the end loop and the first stem. Continue to coil around the base wire and the upright stems to reinforce them. Every few wraps, add a round green bead and wrap so that it sits against the front of the base. Carry on wrapping and adding beads until you have covered the base halfway between the last stem and the end loop. Cut and tuck the wire using wire cutters.

FALL INSPIRATIONS

Fall ushers in crisp mornings, first frosts, and a landscape colored by intense shades of russets and browns. It is a time of abundance, of fruitfulness, but also a time when nature's harvest and the first gales begin to strip the trees of their leaves.

Dandelion clocks launch floating fairy seeds and frost transforms late blooms into sugared roses. Berries cluster in hedgerows and swathes of turning leaves rustle in the trees. Crisp, clear evenings herald dramatic fiery sunsets.

The reds and browns of turning leaves and dramatic sunsets are conveyed to great effect in the oak leaf necklace and the fall leaves and sunset bracelets. The frozen rose bracelet echoes the first cold snap of the season.

SUNSET BRACELET

Stark bare branches are silhouetted against the stunning, vibrant colors of Fall sunsets. Molten lava reds resembling a rare and unusual veined gemstone are preserved under resin for this simply designed, delicate bracelet.

- Photographs of silhouetted trees to set in resin
- Gloss sealer spray or brush-on sealant
- Glue for paper or card
- Two-part resin
- Popsicle stick
- Emery board
- Two-part epoxy glue
- Cocktail stick
- 3 x brass connectors, 18mm
- 3 x brass bezel pans, 18mm
- 3 x four-pronged brass settings, 16mm
- 6in (150mm) length of raw brass filigree peanut chain
- Peanut chain links used for jumprings
- 1 x brass foldover clasp

- Wire cutters
- Scissors
- Nylon jaw pliers
- Chain-nose pliers
- Bent-nose pliers
- Flat-nose pliers

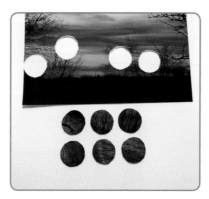

1 Choose the sections of photograph you plan to use and draw around a template using a ballpoint pen. Seal the areas with gloss sealer spray or paint sealer on using a brush. When dry, cut out using sharp scissors. Glue the photos into the bezel pans—any glue for card or paper will work fine.

2 Following the steps on pages 36–37 (see also the steps for the Pink blossom bracelet, pages 48–51), mix the resin and add slowly to cover the photo in the bezel. Cover to avoid dust settling in the resin while drying and leave for at least 12 hours. Sand down the metal components that will be glued together, the back of the bezel pans (once the resin is dry!), the four-pronged settings, and the 18mm brass connectors—this gives the glue some "key" to grip to on the shiny surfaces. An emery board is small enough to be used accurately.

For a longer bracelet, use six resin connectors instead of three, or use the same technique to make a pendant.

3 Mix a small amount of two-part epoxy glue, following the manufacturer's instructions. Apply with a cocktail stick and layer the four-pronged setting onto the 18mm brass connector and then glue the bezel pan on top. Depending on the glue brand, you should have a few minutes to adjust the positioning. Once the glue is fully dry, using nylon jaw pliers, press the prongs into the center and flatten. Do opposite prongs two at a time, then press from the sides to lie flat against the resin. Nylon jaw pliers stop the resin from getting scratched.

Resist the temptation to poke the resin to see whether it has set. If you accidentally leave fingerprints or marks in the surface that remain once it is dry, a few drops of freshly mixed resin over the top should restore it to a shiny finish again.

4 Using bent-nose and chain-nose pliers, fasten the three sections together using four chain links as jumprings between the loops on each connector.

5 Add a short length of filigree peanut chain onto the loop on an 18mm brass connector and attach a foldover clasp (or any type of clasp of your choice) using a jumpring.

6 Fasten the opposite side chain length to the loop using a chain link or a jumpring. Add a wrapped loop bead dangle to the last chain link.

DANDELION WISHES PENDANT

Catch a "fairy" seed floating in the air and make a wish! This whimsical bottle pendant filled with "wishes" is a simple project; it is strung onto a green chain with sparkly crackle beads in pale green and sky blue shades to complement.

- Dandelion seeds (or any items you wish to place inside the bottle)
- 1 x tiny bottle and cork stopper, 22mm
- 4 x two-tone blue/green crackle beads, 8mm
- Length of small oval chain in green
- US 20-gauge (SWG 21, 0.8mm) green wire
- US 18-gauge (SWG 19, 1mm) green wire
- Glue

- Tweezers
- Wire cutters
- Chain-nose pliers
- Round-nose pliers
- Bent-nose pliers
- Flat-nose pliers

1 Fill the tiny bottle with your chosen items. I used tweezers to place the dandelion seeds inside.

2 Glue the cork stopper in place to stop the contents escaping. Leave to dry. Cut a 3in (75mm) length of US 18-gauge (SWG 19, 1mm) wire. Make a wrapped loop (see page 24) at one end and wrap firmly around the bottle's neck to make a bail for the bottle to hang from.

Use rubber coating solution on plier jaws when working with color-coated wire; this prevents the wire becoming marked and showing the inner copper core.

3 Make a hook and eye clasp (see pages 26–27) using US 18-gauge (SWG 19, 1mm) wire. Attach to each end of a 26in (660mm) length of chain and cut chain in half once secured.

4 Cut four 3in (75mm) pieces of US 20-gauge (SWG 21, 0.8mm) wire and thread an 8mm crackle bead onto each. Wrap a loop at one end of each one and leave the other end open after turning the loops.

5 Thread the open loop onto the chain ends and finish making the wrapped loop. Attach the beads together and complete the loops to secure. You could bead as much of the chain as you wish at this stage.

6 Fasten the bead loops on the end to the bottle pendant using a chain link. If the links on your chain are soldered and will not open and close, use a jumpring instead.

FROZEN ROSE BRACELET

A cold-weather snap confuses the garden, and roses in bloom are frosted with ice. For this simple memory wire bracelet, I used sparkly polymer clay roses, icy lampwork beads, and glass beads all in sour pink shades.

1 Cut the US 18-gauge (SWG 19, 1mm) square wire into three lengths of 8in (200mm) and wrap a short length of US 20-gauge (21 SWG, 0.8mm) square wire around to secure. Repeat twice, spacing the wraps in the middle and near each end. Use masking tape to hold it together while you coil around it. Trim all wire ends with wire cutters and tuck in neatly.

3 Form the loop of a wrapped loop (see page 24) on the center wire and thread the hook-and-eye clasp attachment loops directly onto it. Finish the wrapped loop, trim the wire, and tuck ends in neatly.

2 With round-nose pliers, curl the two outer wires into a spiral. Repeat for both sides. Make a right-angle bend in the center wire using chain-nose pliers.

4 You now have a basic wire bracelet form ready to add on wired-on leaves (or any embellishment you choose).

5 Using 12in (305mm) sections of 22-gauge (SWG 23, 0.6mm) orange-colored wire, thread one 8mm goldstone bead to the center of the wire, and twist to secure in place. Thread on the leaves. Add a hole at the tip of the leaves (using a hole punch) so the wire will run up the back, out through the hole, over the leaf, and down the back. Twist at the base of the leaf.

For a coordinated look, try using all the same color wire in different gauges. You can make your wire wrapping as neat or as organic-looking as you like.

6 Repeat step 5 to make the leaf sections ready to attach to the bracelet base. Leave the wire tails under the leaves, as these will be used to fasten the leaves on.

7 Starting at one side, sit the leaf sections so the tail wires are on both sides of the bracelet base. Wrap in opposite directions around the wire, securing the leaf stems as you encounter them.

8 Continue along the bracelet base, adding the leaves and wrapping to secure them into place. Do not worry at this stage about arranging the leaves, as you will need to move them slightly to allow the wire to be wrapped tightly around the base. Cut all wire ends and tuck them tightly onto the reverse of the base. If they still catch, a dab of glue helps.

9 Cut a 24in (610mm) length of 22-gauge (SWG 23, 0.6mm) bronze wire. At one end of the bracelet, under where the leaves begin, attach the wire by wrapping tightly several times. Continue to wrap along the base in between the leaves, adding 4mm brown beads by threading them on and wrapping tightly. When you reach the other side, wrap around the wire again, trim and tuck in the ends as before.

OAK LEAF AND ACORNS NECKLACE

I love fall shades, and in this necklace I played on the difference in textures between the smooth acorn, the rugged acorn cup, and the clusters of ash and sycamore spinners that I loved to play with as a child.

YOU WILL NEED

- Two-part silicone putty
- Two-part resin clay
- Emery board or sandpaper
- Dust mask and goggles for sanding
- Nitrile disposable gloves
- 1 x large copper-plated brass oak leaf, 60 x 25mm (you will need to punch a hanging hole)
- 13 x copper-plated brass leaf stampings, 10 x 30mm
- 14 x copper-plated brass leaf stampings, 25 x 20mm
- 4 x tiny acorn copper-plated brass stampings (2 used on acorn cluster)
- 2 x small oak leaf stampings (add a central hole in one for clasp)
- 12 x assorted glass or acrylic seed-like beads in shades of brown, various sizes

- 2 x brecciated jasper ovals, 30 x 15mm
- 19in (480mm) length of chain
- US 22-gauge (SWG 23, 0.6mm) bronze wire (for sycamore seed loops and bead connectors)
- 2 x brass acorn cup bead caps
- Jumprings, 5mm
- 1 x jumpring, 10mm
- 8 x ball-end headpins for seed-like bead dangles
- Large leaf toggle clasp
- Bronze metal paint
- Sealer
- Cocktail stick
- Flat-nose pliers
- Round-nose pliers
- Bent-nose pliers
- Wire cutters
- Hole punch

1 Make silicon molds of an acorn, an acorn cup, and a sycamore spinner seed (see pages 32–33).

2 Once the molds have dried, remove the acorn, cup, and spinner. Try to remove any debris stuck inside them, otherwise this will be replicated in the molded piece.

Silicone molds are very durable; they can last for many uses if you are gentle when removing molded objects. If you have a precious item then make a spare mold in case the first gets torn or worn.

3 Mix two-part resin clay and add to molds to make your components (see pages 34–35). Usually you would leave the pieces to dry in the mold for 24 hours, but for making multiples quickly flip the clay out and lay flat to dry on waxed paper.

4 Insert a wrapped loop (see page 24) made using US 22-gauge (SWG 23, 0.6mm) wire and twist into the sycamore seeds. Make a slight bend in one wire tail so the loop cannot pull back out. You can carefully remove excess resin clay at this stage by using a blade, pointed tool, or cocktail stick to gently nudge away the overhangs from the molding process. This saves the time and effort of a lot of sanding down.

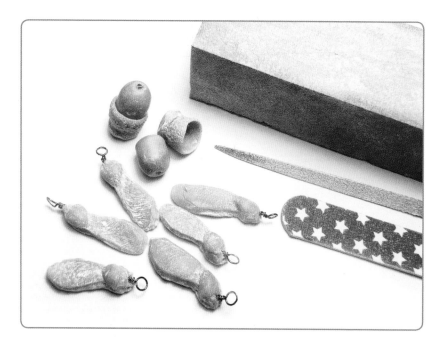

5 Once fully dry and set hard, sand down and remove any excess. Use a file, emery board, sandpaper, or nail buffer block and be sure to wear protective gear—the dust is very fine.

6 Glue the acorns into the cups. Then make an oval-shaped resin clay flat base, press the acorns and cups into place, and add the small leaf and tiny acorn stampings. Make a hanging hole using a cocktail stick and leave the base to dry. Wipe away any dust and paint the seeds, acorns, and base with bronze metal paint. Seal with sealer once dry.

7 Make a selection of wrapped loop beaded connector sections and drops (see page 25) using the seed-shaped beads on ball-end headpins, brecciated jasper ovals, and US 22-gauge (SWG 23, 0.6mm) wire. Attach the metal leaf dangles and beaded loops along the chain length, adding sycamore seeds in clusters of three, and attaching them using 5mm jumprings.

8 Affix chain ends to the acorn cluster using a 10mm jumpring. Add the brecciated jasper ovals and then attach the chain to those and fasten the large oak leaf to the central large jumpring.

9 Add a clasp of your choice. I used a large leaf toggle and a small oak leaf with a central hole punched using a hole punch.

WINTER INSPIRATIONS

In winter, icy, bleak, and bitterly cold weather marks a landscape of naked branches glittering and sparkling with frost and snow. But forsythia brings a welcome burst of color and hardy snowdrops hint that spring is on its way again.

Glossy red berries contrast with sunny blue skies and crisp snow. A sharp cold snap coats the landscape in spiky fairyland frost. Spiderwebs catch crystal dewdrops. Forsythia in bloom and resilient snowdrops herald the end of winter.

From the hoar frost necklace to the snowdrop earrings, the winter projects reflect the frozen, crystalline nature of the season. The snowy holly bag charm and the forsythia brooch bring splashes of color to a wintry wardrobe.

SNOWY HOLLY
BAG CHARM

Crisp, snow-laden holly leaves sparkle in the winter sun and red berries glisten. That was the inspiration for this bag charm, with its luscious berry reds, festive green holly and ivy leaves, and pristine white beads dangling above a large brass holly leaf.

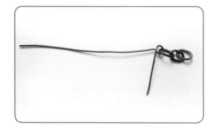

1 Undo some of the chain into three-link sections; keep the links that are opened to use as jumprings later. Take a 3in (75mm) piece of US 20-gauge (SWG 21, 0.8mm) wire and make the start of a wrapped loop (see page 24) using chain-nose and round-nose pliers. Slip one of the chain sections into the loop before continuing to wrap it closed.

2 Add beads to the wire and repeat at the other end, adding a three-link section of chain before closing the loop.

3 Continue adding chain and beaded connectors until the sides of the necklace are the desired length.

4 To make the centerpiece rosehip dangle, add the polymer clay rosehips onto headpins and make wrapped loops. On one, add a dog bone connector and a 4mm spacer bead to stagger the height that they hang. Also make wrapped loop dangles with three frosty red/green 8mm jade beads. Add all dangles onto a 10mm jumpring.

6 Divide the remaining length of chain into two equal parts. Open the end link and attach to the necklace sides. Fasten a toggle clasp to the chain ends.

5 Assemble more wrapped loop dangles to hang in clusters of three. Attach using chain links to the main necklace body on the top link of each three-link section.

Beaded chains can be made with as many links of chain and bead connectors as you wish; you can also vary the lengths of the chain segments in between the beads for many possible combinations.

HOAR FROST NECKLACE

Every branch and twig in the garden is covered with the most delicate shards of hoar frost, beautiful and sparkly. To recreate that glittering ice, I used all frosted and crystal beads for this necklace, along with some icy lampwork beads made especially.

YOU WILL NEED

- 21 x frosted acrylic leaves, 25mm
- 7 x icy lampwork rondelle beads, 14mm (mine were specially commissioned, but any crystal rondelles would work)
- 3 x round frosted white glass bases (you could also use metal filigree or buttons)
- 1 x crescent brass base in heavy-gauge raw brass, 4½in/115mm
- 11 x frosted Czech glass leaves with AB ("aurora borealis") finish, 12 x 10mm
- 4 x faceted round crystal beads, 6mm
- 4 x crystal bicones, 4mm
- 4 x tube faceted crystal beads, 12 x 6mm (for chain section)

- Clear seed beads, 2mm
- 2 x Czech glass rough-cut faceted beads, 12mm
- 35 x clear quartz chip beads
- 10in (250mm) length of medium curb chain in white
- US 20-gauge (SWG 21, 0.8mm) silver wire
- US 24-gauge (SWG 25, 0.5mm) silver wire
- 6 x ball-end headpin, 50mm
- 1 x lobster clasp
- Glue

- Screw-type hole punch
- Wire cutters
- Round-nose pliers
- Chain-nose pliers
- Bent-nose pliers
- Flat-nose pliers

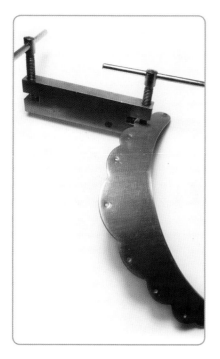

1 Punch holes spaced along the brass crescent base; along the fluted, scalloped edges make attachment points for wiring later. Use a manual screw-type hole punch or an electric drill.

2 Cut 3in (75mm) lengths of US 20-gauge (SWG 21, 0.8mm) wire using wire cutters. Turn a loop at one end with the smallest part of the jaws of a pair of round-nose pliers. Thread onto the wire a lampwork icy bead (the loop will prevent it slipping through), three acrylic leaves, and a large round frosted glass base. Turn a loop using round-nose pliers on the reverse to secure and twist the loop (like a button shank) so that the wire can pass through.

3 With a 12in (305mm) length of US 20-gauge (SWG 21, 0.8mm) wire, pass through the loop on the reverse of the flower and wrap tightly around the crescent brass base, wrap several times, and tuck in the wire ends. Use the scallop edge on the base as an anchor point.

4 Repeat steps 2 and 3 to make and attach three main flowers on the base.

5 Add three AB-finish glass leaves onto a 50mm ball-end headpin and turn into a circle. Thread the wire end to and fro through the center to keep the circular petal shape. Twist and coil the wire end of the headpin and tuck in ends neatly. Thread onto another headpin with leaves and coil at reverse to secure.

6 Repeat step 5 to make another flower with AB leaves. Wire both to the base using the same method as in step 3.

To hold wired-on objects more firmly to bases, first flatten the wraps with flat-nose pliers and then make a twist in each wire on the reverse; this makes the wires tighten. If there is still "play," a dab of glue on the reverse helps. Do this last, as gaps are useful to attach other wire to as you add elements to the necklace. The reverse of the base could be covered with faux suede or ribbon if preferred, but as long as the wire wraps are flat and the ends tucked in then they won't snag.

7 Add any extra acrylic leaves and AB glass leaves in the spaces. Glue into place (clamp into place if needed) and allow to dry for 24 hours.

8 Attach a 12in (305mm) length of US 24-gauge (SWG 25, 0.5mm) wire to the reverse of the base at one end. String 2mm beads along the wire and wrap it in the spaces between the large flowers, anchoring it as you go along by wrapping in attachment wires and holes. Thread on quartz chips and sparkly glass beads, making slight loops that hang down below the flowers.

9 Wire as before from the opposite end, again adding beads into the spaces and passing the wire in the gap between the flowers. Construct a beaded chain from wrapped looped connectors (see page 25) and add a length of chain to make the necklace the desired length. Finally, add a simple lobster clasp.

SPIDERWEB NECKLACE

Spiderwebs covered in dew are the prettiest little jewels, strung out like tiny lights along the strands, and sparkling in the sunlight. For this multi-strand necklace, I used quartz beads strung on "invisible" thread to catch the light.

YOU WILL NEED

- 78 x clear quartz round beads, 2mm
- 15 x clear quartz round beads, 4mm
- Invisible nylon thread
- Short length of fine chain
- 2 x wire guardians
- 1 x lobster clasp
- 3 x jumprings, 4mm
- Crimps
- Crimp covers

- Crimping pliers
- Foldback clip or small clamp
- Beading needle
- Needle threader
- Wire cutters
- Chain-nose pliers
- Bent-nose pliers

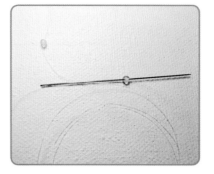

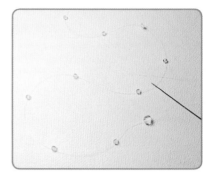

1 Use a needle threader to thread the needle with nylon invisible thread. Be generous with the length, as you can always cut off any excess afterward. Make five strands in staggered lengths so that they drape nicely when worn. Thread a 2mm bead, run it to about 6in (150mm) of the thread end, and then loop the needle back through the bead again; this holds the bead in place. Repeat for each bead added.

2 For three of the strands, add nine x 2mm beads, three x 4mm, and then nine x 2mm again. The next strand has seven x 2mm, then three x 4mm, then seven x 2mm again. The fifth and shortest strand has five x 2mm beads, three x 4mm, and then five x 2mm.

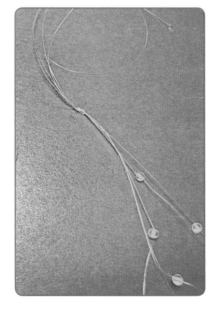

3 When you have added all the beads, gather the ends of the thread together and tie an overhand knot to secure on each side. This step is shown on a dark background, as clear thread on a white backdrop is hard to see!

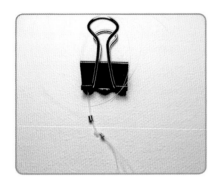

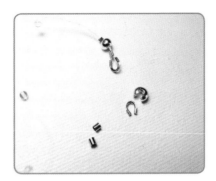

4 Slip a crimp bead down along the loose thread ends, over the knot. Using crimping pliers, squash and fold it to secure. Add another crimp bead above the knot. Secure with a foldback clip while you do the same on the other side.

5 Thread the loose thread ends through the wire guardian. It helps if the ends are not trimmed to the same length at this stage and can be put through the holes one at a time. As the threads poke out of the second hole of the wire guardian, feed them into the crimp bead. When all five threads are through, crimp as before to secure. Trim any excess thread using wire cutters.

6 Add crimp covers to cover up the knots and also over the crimps if preferred. Hold the crimp cover in chain-nose pliers, slide over the knot, and squeeze closed. Use round-nose and bent-nose pliers to attach the chain length and clasp to the wire guardian loops.

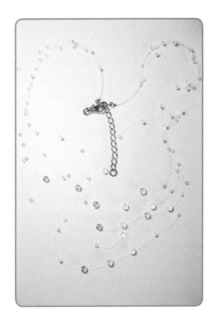

Work in a good light when using invisible thread, as the combination of tiny beads and fine thread can be challenging. You will definitely want to use a needle threader to preserve your sanity, as the holes in fine beading needles are very small—a regular sewing one is fine.

FORSYTHIA BROOCH

These cheery yellow flowers crowd together on otherwise bare branches and hint that winter may be coming to an end. I used Czech glass mustard-yellow leaves as petals for this brooch, with briolettes for raindrops and tiny seed beads as a background.

YOU WILL NEED

- 4 x Czech glass leaves (use as petals), 14 x 9mm
- 1 x Czech glass bell flower, 6mm
- 3 x clear crystal briolettes, 6mm
- 1 x yellow seed bead, 2mm (for center of flower)
- 2mm and 3mm seed beads in lichen shades (gray, green, and yellow)
- Invisible nylon thread
- US 24-gauge (SWG 25, 0.5mm) brown wire
- 2 x perforated oval brass dapped shapes, 20 x 30mm
- 1 x brooch pin, 20mm

- Flat-nose or chain-nose pliers
- Wire cutters
- Glue
- Fine beading needle
- Needle threader
- Third hand clip stand (optional)

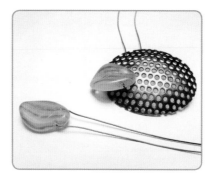

1 Thread one of the petal beads with US 24-gauge (SWG 25, 0.5mm) wire and loop the wire ends through two holes on the perforated oval base. Twist the wire on the reverse to secure into place. Do not over-twist, as the wire is delicate and may snap.

2 Loop wire through the bell flower; include a yellow seed bead so that the wire cannot pass through the bell-flower bead center.

3 Secure the bell-flower center adjacent to the petal and twist on the back of the base as before. Then add the other three petals of the flower in the same way. Twist the wires together on the back, trim off any excess, and press flat to the reverse of the base. These wire ends will be hidden once the back section is added.

4 The flower petals can be adjusted for positioning. Take care not to break the securing wires.

5 Thread the clear crystal raindrop beads using the same method as the petals, and attach to the perforated oval.

6 Attach all three raindrops, then twist and trim the wires on the reverse using pliers and wire cutters and tuck flat against the base.

A sieve-top brooch finding could be used instead of the perforated oval bases.

7 Thread up a fine beading needle with invisible thread; using a needle threader helps greatly as the needle eye is tiny. Make a knot and add a seed bead to the reverse to prevent thread pulling through the perforated base. Add the seed beads to fill in the holes, threading to and fro the base until it is covered. Knot on the reverse to secure.

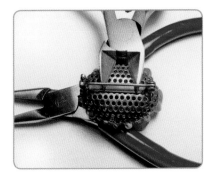

8 Glue the brooch setting to the second perforated base, which will form the back of the brooch. Using a third hand clip stand is useful to keep the base level while the glue dries.

9 Glue the two base sections together; apply glue to the base perimeters only as the middle sections will not touch due to the curves. The wirework and thread will be hidden inside neatly. Use pliers or any other objects for support while the glue is drying.

SNOWDROP EARRINGS

Understated and delicate, the "fair maid of February" is one of the few flowers to withstand snow's icy touch. I used white petal-shaped beads to make these pretty drop earrings; glass dagger-shaped beads would also work well.

YOU WILL NEED

- 6 x petal-shaped white glass beads, 15 x 9mm
- 2 x white acrylic bell-shaped flowers, 10mm
- 2 x white seed beads, 3mm
- 6 x moss agate round beads, 4mm
- US 20-gauge (SWG 21, 0.8mm) wire in green
- US 28-gauge (SWG 30, 0.3mm) wire in green
- 0.8mm-diameter clear elastic
- 1 x silver headpin, 50mm
- Sandpaper or file
- Instant glue

- Wire cutters
- Chain-nose pliers
- Bent-nose pliers
- Nylon jaw pliers
- Round-nose pliers

1 Cut a 2in (50mm) piece of US 28-gauge (SWG 30, 0.3mm) wire using wire cutters. With your fingers, coil it around a 3in (75mm) length of US 20-gauge (SWG 21, 0.8mm) wire; coil seven times. Slide from the end of the US 20-gauge (SWG 21, 0.8mm) wire. Do this twice.

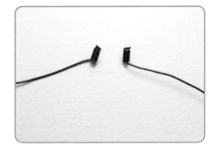

2 Trim the ends of the coiled wire. Leave tails on one end for now to make it easier to handle these tiny, springy coils.

3 Cut two 2in (50mm) pieces of 20-gauge (SWG 21, 0.8mm) wire. Using the smallest part of the jaws of a pair of round-nose pliers, turn a loop and bend it slightly to center the loop above the wire tail.

You can make ear wires to match any color scheme. Usually the core of the wire is copper, so handle it gently to avoid marring the colored coating.

4 Add a 4mm moss agate bead above the loop; carefully slide the wire coils above this and squeeze gently against the US 20-gauge (SWG 21, 0.8mm) central wire. Trim the wire tails and press firmly against the larger wire.

5 Above the coiled wire section, make a slight angled bend using chain-nose pliers. Then, using the largest part of the round-nose pliers, bend the wire into a gentle curve.

6 Repeat for the second earring, gently smoothing the wire around the round-nose pliers' jaw to make the earring hoop section. Sand or file away any sharp wire ends.

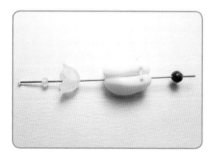

7 Thread the three petal-shaped white beads onto a 3in (75mm) length of 0.8mm-diameter elastic. Tie a reef knot and pull the ends tightly to make sure the knot is secure. Dab some instant glue onto the knot and allow it to dry. Trim any excess elastic using wire cutters or sharp scissors.

8 Thread a 50mm headpin, with a seed bead, an acrylic bell flower, the three petals on elastic, and a moss agate 4mm bead. Press firmly into place. Add a dab of instant glue under the moss agate 4mm bead, and make sure the petal beads are central and evenly spread. Clamp until the glue has dried.

9 Make a wire coil as before (step 1), with more coils this time. Slide the coil above the moss agate 4mm bead and add another 4mm bead. Turn a loop using round-nose pliers at the end of the headpin and trim. Press in any wire ends on the coil using chain-nose pliers. Attach to the earring wire by opening the loop and closing it with pliers.

SUPPLIERS

All the materials and supplies used are listed with each project. Below is a list of suppliers for some of those items. If you have trouble locating a particular item, a quick search online should be rewarding. Where I have used vintage or repurposed beads, feel free to substitute your own choice of beads.

Alchemy & Ice
www.alchemyandice.com
For beads, wire, findings, tools, resin, and silicone molding putty.

Beadazzled by Elise
www.beadazzledbyelise.com
For polymer clay flowers handmade by Elise Canning.

B'Sue Boutiques
www.bsueboutiques.com
For brass stampings, wire, sari ribbon, cameos, findings, settings, Swellegant dye oxide, and patina.

Delphine's Flower Bead Shop
www.delphinesflowerbeadshop.com
For acrylic flowers.

The Fyre Faerie
www.etsy.com/shop/TheFyreFaerie
For handmade glass lampwork beads.

JHT Taxidermy Supplies
www.stores.ebay.co.uk/JHT-Taxidermy-Supplies
For Apoxie Sculpt two-part resin clay.

Sunny Beads North East
www.sunnyenterprise.co.uk
For semi-precious and glass beads.

ACKNOWLEDGMENTS

Author's Acknowledgments

I would like to express my gratitude to those who encouraged, supported, and believed in me while I worked on this book.

Thanks to GMC Publications for allowing me to make the dream a reality; to Sara Harper, my project editor, and the rest of the team for all the help and work they put in to bringing the book forth to fruition.

Thank you to my family and friends, for indulging my whimsical notions, tolerating the hours spent interpreting those into actual projects, and letting me "think aloud" constantly!

Thanks to my children for putting up with all the burned teas while I worked, and for living knee-deep in beads.

Brenda-Sue Lansdowne—who I am proud to call my friend—for inspiring me, and encouraging me to follow my dreams.

My social media group of like-minded friends for preserving my sanity.

And to my parents for the creative and "book-writing" genes, and for giving me my first camera on my eighth birthday.

Picture Credits

All photography by the author, except for the following: Pages 49, 89, 101, 141: Rebecca Mothersole/GMC. Page 42: Artwork Gilda Pacitti/GMC; (top left): *Daffodils* Berthe Morisot/WikiPaintings; (top right) *Bluebells* USSR stamp S. V. Gerasimov/Wikimedia Commons. Page 43: (top) *The Lavalier* Guy Rose/WikiPaintings; (middle) *Blossoming Almond Branch in a Glass with a Book* Vincent van Gogh/Wikimedia Commons. Page 72: Artwork Gilda Pacitti/GMC; (bottom left) Wikimedia Commons; (bottom right) *Shinnecock Hills* William Merritt Chase/WikiPaintings. Page 73: (top left) Wikimedia Commons; (top right) *Flower Still Life* Jan van Huysum/Wikimedia Commons. Page 106: Artwork; Gilda Pacitti/GMC; (left) *Autumn Leaves* John Everett Millais/Wikimedia Commons; (right) *Still Life with Flowers and Fruit* Claude Monet. Page 107: (top left) *The White Birch* Axel Törneman/Wikimedia Commons; (bottom) *Herbstlandschaft mit Kühen* Richard von Poschinger/Wikimedia Commons. Page 138: Artwork Gilda Pacitti/GMC; (left) *Snow at Louveciennes* Alfred Sisley/Wikimedia Commons; (right) *Hare in the Snow* Ferdinand von Rayski/Wikimedia Commons; (bottom) *Snowdrops* USSR stamp Wikimedia Commons. Page 139: (bottom) *Hunters in the Snow (Winter)* Pieter Bruegel the Elder/Wikimedia Commons.

INDEX

acrylic flowers 20
adhesives 18–19

bead caps 15
beading needles 17
beading wire 17
beads 19–20
Bee and aquilegia necklace 74–7
bent-nose pliers 11
Bleeding heart bracelet 56–9
Bluebell bracelet 60–63
Buttercups and daisies bracelet 78–81
Butterflies and thistles tiara 100–103

cabochons 20
casts 34–5
chain 16
chain-nose pliers 10
Chain Sta grips 12
clasps 15
connectors 15, 25
crimp pliers 12
crimps 28–9

Daffodil necklace 44–7
Dandelion wishes pendant 112–15
double-end connectors 25
Dragonfly woods necklace 82–7
dye oxide paints 38–9

earring findings 15

Fall leaves bracelet 124–9
findings 14–15
flat nose pliers 10
Forget-me-not necklace 64–9
Forsythia brooch 158–61
found materials 21
Frozen berries necklace 144–7
Frozen rose bracelet 116–19
Fruits and berries lariat 120–23

headpins 14
heat gun 12
heatproof cloth 13
Hoar frost necklace 148–53
hole punches 12
hook and eye clasps 26–7

inspiration 22–3

jumprings 14

Magnolia necklace 52–5
memory wire 16
memory wire cutters 11
molds 32–3
monofilament 17

nylon jaw pliers 11

Oak leaf and acorns necklace 130–35

Pink blossom bracelet 48–51
planning 22–3
pliers 10, 11, 12

resin 36–7
ribbon 17
Rose cameo choker 94–9
round-nose pliers 11

sealants 19
shrink plastic 30–31
Snowy holly bag charm 140–43
Snowdrop earrings 162–5
soldering block 13
Spiderweb necklace 154–7
stampings 20
Storm clouds necklace 88–93
Sunset bracelet 108–11

third hand clip stand 12
tweezers 13

wire 16–17
wire cutters 11
wrapped loops 24

**To place an order,
or to request a catalog, contact:**

GMC Publications, Castle Place, 166 High Street,
Lewes, East Sussex BN7 1XU United Kingdom
Tel: +44 (0)1273 488005 www.gmcbooks.com